MACMILLA[illegible]

ELEMENT[illegible]

ARTHUR C. CLARKE

Tales of Ten Worlds

Retold by Helen Reid-Thomas

MACMILLAN

MACMILLAN READERS

ELEMENTARY LEVEL

Founding Editor: John Milne

The Macmillan Readers provide a choice of enjoyable reading materials for learners of English. The series is published at six levels – Starter, Beginner, Elementary, Pre-Intermediate, Intermediate and Upper.

Level control

Information, structure and vocabulary are controlled to suit the students' ability at each level.

The number of words at each level:

Starter	about 300 basic words
Beginner	about 600 basic words
Elementary	about 1100 basic words
Pre-Intermediate	about 1400 basic words
Intermediate	about 1600 basic words
Upper	about 2200 basic words

Vocabulary

Some difficult words and phrases in this book are important for understanding the story. Some of these words are explained in the story and some are shown in the pictures. From Pre-Intermediate level upwards, words are marked with a number like this: ...[3]. These words are explained in the Glossary at the end of the book.

Contents

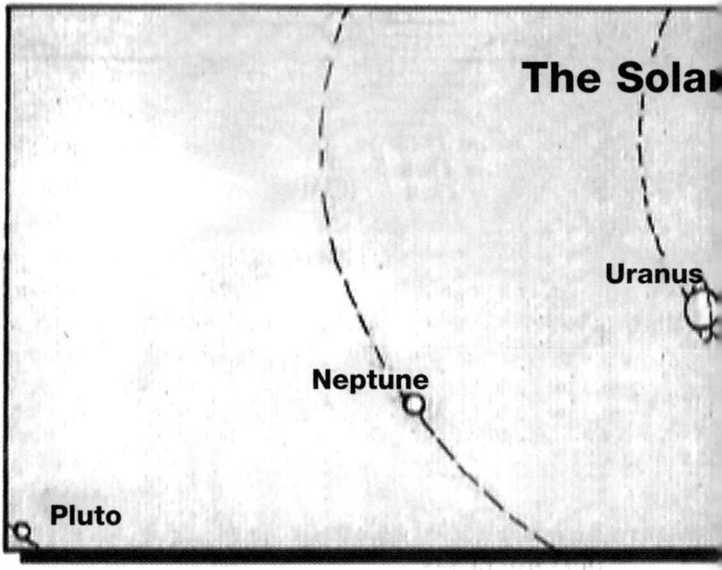

A Note About These Stories

Arthur C. Clarke, the writer of these ten stories, is a famous writer of science fiction stories. In a science-fiction story, the writer imagines what the world will be like in the future.

The writer imagines that spaceships have been invented which carry passengers on long voyages through space. The writer also imagines that space stations and laboratories have been built on the Moon and other planets. When space travellers go outside a space station, they have to wear spacesuits. Spacesuits make it possible for the wearers to breathe, and also they protect the wearers from great heat or great cold.

The stories in this collection are set in many different

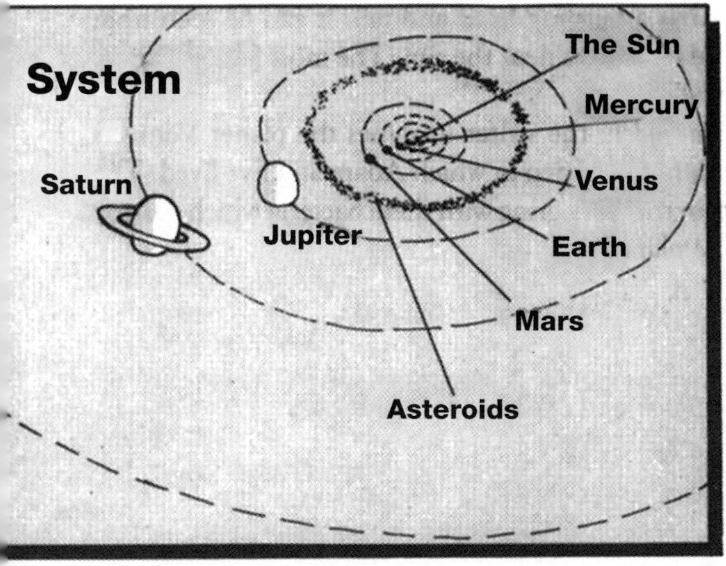

places. Two are set on Earth and the others are set in space. Most of the people in the stories are scientists who travel in space to find out more about the planets and the stars. But some of the characters are astronomers. Astronomers study space by looking through telescopes. A telescope makes it possible for an astronomer to see stars and planets which are far away from Earth.

Summertime on Icarus is about an accident to a space pod – a small spaceship. The accident happens on an asteroid. An asteroid is a very small planet which goes round the sun between Mars and Jupiter. Another story, *Who's There?* is set in a space station – a large satellite going round the Earth twenty thousand miles out in space. And *Dog Star* is a story set in a laboratory on the Moon.

Into the Comet is set in a spaceship travelling in the tail of a comet. A comet is an object which travels through space.

A comet has a burning head and tail. It can be seen from Earth when it travels near the sun. The most famous comet is Halley's Comet.

In *Before Eden*, the writer imagines the planet Venus is like the Garden of Eden in which Adam and Eve lived. The scientists in the story bring with them bacteria which destroy life on the planet.

SUMMERTIME ON ICARUS

Colin Sherrard opened his eyes. He looked up and saw the sky. It was black and crowded with stars.

Where am I? he asked himself.

Then he remembered. He was in his space pod and it had crashed. It had crashed on Icarus, the hottest place in the solar system. Icarus was an asteroid. Icarus was the nearest asteroid to the sun. Colin Sherrard was nearer the sun than any man had ever been before.

Sherrard was lying in his damaged space pod. The pod had crashed among huge rough rocks on Icarus on a world only two miles in diameter. At that moment, it was night where he was. And in the darkness it was cold. But it was a very short night – it lasted only four hours. In four hours' time, Sherrard thought, my pod will be facing the sun. It will be in the middle of a burning fire. And I will be inside it.

Sherrard looked out into space. He saw one star brighter than the rest. But it wasn't a star. He knew that it wasn't a star. It was the light from *Prometheus*. *Prometheus* was the spaceship that had brought him to Icarus, across millions of miles of space.

He sat up. He knew now where he was. He remembered what had happened. He was working with other scientists on Icarus. They were trying to find out more about the sun. They always worked at night because it was cooler then. They placed scientific instruments on the rocks. Then they covered the instruments with metal foil. The thin metal foil protected the instruments from the burning daytime sun.

After a short time, the other scientists went back to

Prometheus. But Sherrard stayed to finish the work. When he was ready to leave, he sent a message to *Prometheus*.

'I'm leaving now,' he told the captain of the spaceship. 'I'll be back in five minutes.'

He aimed the pod at the spaceship. There was a loud explosion. Immediately he knew that something was wrong. The pod shot off the asteroid in the wrong direction and began spinning out of control.

He tried to get the pod back on course, but the controls did not work. Then he remembered something he read long ago: 'If you don't know what to do, do nothing.' So he waited and did nothing.

The pod spun round and round. Suddenly he saw the black rocks of Icarus above his head. The asteroid seemed to fall on top of him. The stars disappeared and his pod crashed onto the rough, black surface.

Fortunately, his pod was not badly damaged. The air supply was still working. He tried to fire the jets again. But they did not work. He tried to contact *Prometheus*. The radio was not working. But the long metal arms of the space pod were still working.

The arms of the pod will save me, he said to himself. I can use them to pull the pod over the rough ground. I must move the pod and stay out of the heat of the sun.

He was sure his friends were coming to rescue him. But until they arrived he would have to keep moving. The shadow of night lasted only four hours on Icarus.

I must move at once, he thought. I must stay in the shadow.

He put his fingers into the controls that worked the metal arms. He moved the arms one at a time. The pod moved – first the right arm, then the left arm. The pod moved like a huge insect across the rough ground. Sherrard began to feel happier. The others will be here soon, he said to himself. I'll be back in time for dinner!

At that moment everything went wrong. Suddenly he was looking down a cliff. He became dizzy. He felt like a fly clinging to a ceiling. He was afraid that he was going to fall off Icarus. He felt he was going to fall into the black spaces between the stars.

His body was covered with sweat and he felt faint. He closed his eyes. The next moment, the pod crashed onto the rocks. He opened his eyes and looked out. He saw in front of him the broken and twisted metal arms of his space pod. He had crashed into a big rock.

Every moment the sun was coming nearer. Sherrard saw the bright light that came from it. He did not feel the heat yet, but he was afraid. He knew that soon the heat would be on him.

I must find shelter, he thought, or I will be burnt alive.

Perhaps there was shelter behind the rock. He used the broken arms to move the pod into the shadow of the rock. He lay there in his space pod.

He looked out into space. Far, far away he saw the beautiful planet Earth. Earth was his home. He did not want to say goodbye to it forever. He did not want to die here on Icarus.

Outside it was growing hotter and brighter every moment. A brilliant flame flashed over the horizon. He felt the burning light of the sun on his legs.

When I feel the full heat of the sun, I will pull the Emergency Lever, thought Sherrard. Then the pod will explode and I will die immediately.

Suddenly he saw a bright flash of light above him.

Suddenly he saw a bright flash of light above him.

It looked like a huge mirror hanging in the sky. The light from the sun was shining on the mirror. He did not understand it. But he had no time to think about it. The heat was getting fiercer. He was unable to bear it.

He put his hand on the red Emergency Lever. He pulled the lever. Nothing happened. The lever did not move. He tried again. Still nothing. Sherrard knew he was going to die. But not quickly and easily. His death was going to be slow and painful under the burning rays of that terrible sun. Suddenly he heard his own voice. He was screaming, screaming with fear.

Then he heard another sound. It was a human voice, and it was calling his name.

'Sherrard,' the voice said. 'Sherrard. We're coming. We're coming to rescue you.'

It was the voice of the captain of the spaceship.

'Save me!' Sherrard shouted. 'I'm here. Quick! I'm being burnt alive!'

There was very little shade left behind the rock. But at that moment, something came between Sherrard and the terrible heat. Its shadow was cool and the bright light no longer hurt his eyes. He looked up and saw a big screen of metal foil above him. There, in its shadow, was another space pod. His friends had come to rescue him!

They picked him up in the broken pod and flew back to *Prometheus*. In his tiny space pod, Sherrard turned and looked again at the planet Earth. He waved his hand towards it.

'Here I am,' he said silently. 'I'm coming home.'

WHO'S THERE?

I work in a space station. From my office, I can see the Earth twenty thousand miles away. It floats in space like a big green and blue ball.

I am the Station Supervisor. I like my job, but I sometimes get bored inside the space station.

One day, I was in my office watching the men working outside. They were building part of the station. Then someone called me on the radio from the Satellite Control Office.

'There's a small echo here on our radar screen. It's about two miles away and it's hardly moving. Can you see what it is?'

I took out my binoculars and looked at the sky. A small satellite was coming towards us. It looked old. I told the man in the Satellite Control Office what I had seen.

'That's dangerous,' he said. 'It will get in the way of our spaceships. Can you go out and bring it in?'

I was pleased to do something different. I didn't get out of the space station very often. My office had a beautiful view, but it was good to get outside.

I put away my papers and went to get my spacesuit. All the spacesuits were kept in large lockers. On my way to the lockers I met our cat, Tommy. Most animals don't like living in space, but Tommy was happy. All the men liked him. As I passed Tommy, he rubbed against my legs. But I was in a hurry and could not stop to talk to him.

I climbed into my spacesuit. It wasn't really a suit. It was more like a tiny spaceship, big enough for one man. I checked the fuel, oxygen, radio and batteries. It was going to be a very short trip, so I didn't check the lockers and the food stores in the suit.

Soon I was out in space. I had to protect my eyes from the sun. In space, the sun's light is dangerous. It is very bright and it can blind you in a second. The spacesuit had a special sunshade for protection.

I saw the satellite and began to move towards it.

This will only take a few minutes, I thought.

But at that moment something went wrong. I heard a noise. It was a strange noise. It was not one of the noises you hear in a spacesuit. It wasn't very loud, but it made me feel afraid.

Then I heard something scraping on the metal of the spacesuit. I froze with fear. The hairs on the back of my neck stood up. Something was outside. And it was something alive.

There's something outside. And it's trying to get into my spacesuit, I thought. What can it be?

Then a name came into my mind.

Bernie Summers! I thought. He died in space. His spacesuit broke open.

After the accident, Bernie Summers' spacesuit had been repaired. Spacesuits were very expensive, so we never threw them away. After an accident, they were repaired and other men used them.

Had Bernie Summers died in this spacesuit? Was his ghost trying to get back into it? I had heard strange stories about ghosts in space. I felt cold sweat on my forehead.

I grew more and more afraid.

I must find out. Is this *Bernie Summers' spacesuit*?

I switched the radio to the emergency station.

I froze with fear. The hairs on the back of my neck stood up.

'Help!' I shouted. 'I'm in trouble! Can you tell me something? Did this spacesuit belong to – '

I never finished the sentence. At that moment, I felt something. Something patted me softly on the back of my neck. I screamed as loud as I could. I pulled myself away from the soft thing and hit my head on the control panel. I fainted and fell forward.

Sometime later, I woke up. I was back in the space station and there was a big bruise on my forehead. The doctors were round my bed. But they weren't looking at me. They were looking at something more interesting. The doctors were playing with three kittens.

Then I remembered the cat, Tommy. I had met Tommy when I was going to get my spacesuit. Tommy? A tom-cat? We had all made a mistake.

Our Tommy wasn't a tom-cat. She was a mother! She had put her babies in the locker in the spacesuit. They had made those strange scratching noises. One of them had patted me on the neck with its soft little paw. I had been knocked out by a kitten!

INTO THE COMET

'I don't know why I'm recording this,' said George Pickett slowly into the microphone. 'No one will ever hear what I am saying. The comet will bring us back to Earth. But the journey will take two million years. The spaceship will be all right then – but we won't!'

'We're trapped in the middle of Randall's Comet. It's like floating in a sea of ice. Great, grey icebergs are moving slowly all around us. Now and again, there are explosions. There is gas in this sea of ice. The gas sometimes explodes with brilliant light. We are travelling in the middle of a fireworks display. It's beautiful, but it's death. We can't get out.'

Six months earlier, George Pickett was chosen to go on the spaceship *Challenger*. A team of men were going to explore Randall's Comet, which no one had ever seen before. The comet appeared in the sky above the Earth every two million years.

Pickett was very pleased to be chosen. He was a journalist. His job on *Challenger* was to interview all the men on the ship and send the recordings back to Earth. But he had to do other jobs on the ship too. He was in charge of the stores and the accounts. Each day he was kept busy all the time. He never had any free time.

But now, he thought, I have too much free time.

A few days earlier, he had counted the stores as usual. He went to check his sums on the computer. The first figures that came up on the screen were wrong. But they were not only wrong – they were terribly wrong. He tried to do

'It's like floating in a sea of ice. Great, grey icebergs are moving slowly all around us.'

the sum again: cans of meat at the beginning of voyage 60, cans of meat used on voyage 17, cans of meat remaining 99999943.

What was going wrong?

He decided to ask Dr Martens, the man in charge of the spaceship's computer.

Dr Martens quickly did a few tests. Each time the computer gave impossible answers.

'It's gone mad,' said Martens. 'It can't do the simplest things. It can't add or subtract.'

'But surely we can put it right?' said Pickett.

Martens shook his head.

'Impossible. It's mixing up all the figures.'

'So what do we do now? What does it mean?' said Pickett.

'It means we're dead. Without the computer, we can't get out of this sea of ice. Without the computer, we can't get back to Earth. We're trapped in Randall's Comet for ever.'

The Captain called the men together and told them about the computer. It was difficult for the men to believe that they were all going to die. There was plenty of food and air. They all went on with their work as usual.

Pickett looked out at the icebergs all around.

Will we still be alive when the ship passes the planet Jupiter? he wondered. I'd like to see Jupiter's moons. They go round and round Jupiter like beads on a wire.

Beads on a wire. That thought had been somewhere in his mind for days. What could it be? A picture came clearly into his mind.

No! he thought. They'll laugh at me.

But the picture stayed in his mind. And Pickett began to think very carefully.

Three days later, he showed a strange looking object of wire and wood to Dr Martens.

'Is this a joke?' asked Martens.

'Listen a moment,' said Pickett. 'My grandmother was Japanese. She taught me to use an abacus. You can use an abacus to do any calculation. Test me. Say two numbers and I'll multiply them.'

'Oh, all right – 856 times 437.'

Pickett's fingers moved the beads quickly. In a few seconds he said, '374 072.'

Martens worked the sum out slowly with a pencil and paper and got it wrong. He tried again, and this time his answer was also 374 072.

'Amazing,' said Martens. 'Can you divide numbers too?'

Pickett showed him. Then he told him his plan. Martens started to smile. Then he laughed – the first laugh on *Challenger* for many days. 'Go ahead,' he said. 'Tell them we're all going to play with beads. I want to see their faces.'

At first, the men did not believe Pickett. But then he showed them how the abacus worked. They began to understand his plan. The engineers made twenty abacuses like Pickett's. Then the classes began. Pickett explained what they had to do. Every day, for hours and hours, everyone on the ship practised using the abacus.

Finally, after days of practice, they were ready.

Martens had a difficult job. He worked out the figures. Then he gave the figures to the men. And they followed his instructions. They were working together like an enormous human computer. Two teams worked separately and they checked each other's results.

Pickett spoke into his recorder.

'We've built a computer out of human beings,' he said. 'We can't get ourselves back to Earth. But we can get near enough to use our radio. Then the computers on Earth will be able to guide us back.

'We've got out of the comet already. I'm glad we won't see those icebergs again.'

'Hello Earth . . . hello Earth Can you hear us? *Challenger* calling. Give us a signal. We're coming home!'

LET THERE BE LIGHT

Edgar Burton and his wife, Mary, were a strange couple. Edgar was twenty years older than his wife. He had made a quarter of a million pounds in business and then he stopped working. There was only one thing that he wanted to do – and that was to study astronomy. He spent all his days making telescopes, and all his nights watching the stars.

Mr and Mrs Burton lived in a fine old house in a lonely part of England. It was beautiful but quiet. Mary was not happy. She had nothing to do. They had servants who did all the housework. There were no neighbours. Mary did not like reading. Her husband spent all his time studying astronomy. Mary Burton's life was very dull.

But one day, she found a new interest. She met a man called Rupert de Vere Courtenay. He was tall and handsome and came from an old and famous family. Mary and Rupert soon got to know each other very well.

Edgar knew that his wife, Mary, was often away from home. But he did not know where she went. He did not know who she met. Then one day, Edgar saw Mary and Rupert in town. They were coming out of the cinema together. At first Edgar was not worried. But the next day Mary told him a lie.

'I couldn't get a ticket for the cinema,' she said, 'so I went to see Mrs Clark instead.'

Edgar at once became suspicious. His wife had told him a lie. He wanted to know the truth. He began to watch Mary carefully. He often saw her with Rupert.

Mary is in love with Rupert, he said to himself.

They were coming out of the cinema together.

Mary went to town twice a week to see Rupert. The road from the Burtons' house to the town was narrow and twisting. Mary always drove back at night very fast along this twisting country road. She was a much faster driver than her husband. From the house, Edgar could see the headlights of the car as they twisted and turned along the road. At one place, the lights disappeared behind a hill. Then the car came round the bend and the headlights shone right into the house. This always made Edgar angry. He was watching the stars, and the bright headlights shone into his telescope.

Edgar was, by this time, a little mad. He did not love Mary any more and he hated anything that stopped him working. He made a plan to murder her. It was a very clever plan.

He bought a big three-foot-wide reflector mirror. He put it up beside his telescope. Then he placed a powerful lamp so that its light shone onto the mirror. When he switched on his lamp, the very bright reflection shone right onto the bend in the road. At this place, the road ran along beside a steep cliff. It was a very dangerous place.

At last everything was ready. Mary had gone into town. She was coming back later that night. Edgar sat by his reflector mirror. He was waiting for the headlights of her car to appear. At last he saw them in the distance. The lights disappeared behind the hill. Then they shone out again on the sharp bend above the cliff. Edgar switched on the lamp. It shone onto the mirror, and the mirror reflected the powerful light onto the road.

Suddenly a light, fifty times brighter than any headlights, shone into the eyes of the driver. After a moment, Edgar switched off the lamp and watched the car's headlights.

The headlights shone out over the side of the road and

Suddenly a light, fifty times brighter than any headlights, shone into the eyes of the driver.

began to fall. Faster and faster they fell. In a few moments, they disappeared below the hill. Edgar could not hear the explosion, but he saw a red glow. It burnt for a few minutes. Edgar watched it, and then, pleased with his night's work, he went to bed.

About an hour later, the phone rang. To his surprise it was Mary. She wanted to ask about Rupert.

Mary had not been in the car. Rupert had been the driver. He had wanted to tell Edgar about Mary and himself. And now he was dead and Mary was alive.

The shock made Edgar completely mad. He was put into a hospital.

Mary was sad about Rupert's death, but she recovered quickly. She sold the lonely house in the country. She went to live in a pretty little house near the sea.

Her new house is near a Naval College and many of the young sailors come to visit her. She does not drive her car any more. There is always someone who wants to drive it for her.

DEATH AND THE SENATOR

Senator Steelman was dying. His doctor had told him that he was a dying man. In six months' time, the Senator would be dead. He had hoped to be the next President of the United States of America. But now there was no future for him at all.

The car was taking him away from the Capitol, away from all the life and business of Government. Senator Steelman tried not to think about his death. Would anyone feel sorry for him? He had many political enemies. They would not be sorry. And what about his family? When had he last seen his grandchildren? He could do something about them. He picked up the car telephone and rang his daughter Irene. She was surprised.

'Will you let me take the children out tomorrow?' the Senator asked. 'I want to take them to the Museum.'

Irene was even more surprised, but she was pleased.

So next day, Senator Steelman took his grandchildren, Susan and Joey, to the Museum.

The children were excited. They asked hundreds of questions. The Senator knew some of the answers. When he didn't know an answer, he made it up. Together they gazed at the bones of a huge animal that lived millions of years ago. The children and the Senator stood together in silence. Millions of years ago, that animal had walked on the land that was now America. Suddenly the Senator felt very small and unimportant.

The next day, the Senator went back to his office. He had a lot of work to finish. Two weeks later, he phoned his wife. She was in Rome. They had not been together for many years. When he saw her beautiful face on the screen, he wanted to be with her again.

The Senator told his wife what the doctor had said. She was shocked at the news. After a few moments of silence she said, 'I'll come at once. I'll start packing now.' Her words made the Senator feel happy.

The Senator did not feel any pain. But he believed his doctor's words. The doctor had said: 'Senator, you have a heart disease. Your heart will not work much longer.'

His wife or his daughter brought Joey and Susan to see him nearly every day. He was planning a holiday for them all. But it took the Senator a long time to finish his work. He had a lot of financial and legal business to do. Every day at his office, visitors were waiting for him.

One day, he had a special visitor. It was Dr Harkness, a very tall and thin man. The Senator invited him into the office.

'Good morning, Doctor,' he said. 'I'm surprised to see you here.' Senator Steelman remembered Dr Harkness very well. Years ago the doctor had asked the Senator for some money. He wanted the money to do some special scientific work. The doctor wanted to do research in space medicine. The Senator remembered that day very well. He had refused to give the doctor any Government money.

The Senator looked up at the doctor. Why had Dr Harkness come to see him after all these years?

Dr Harkness showed the Senator an article in a scientific magazine. The article was written in Russian. The magazine was the USSR *Journal of Space Medicine*.

'But I can't read Russian,' said the Senator. 'What is it about?'

'It's about the Russian Satellite Hospital,' explained Dr Harkness. 'Doctors in Russia think that they can help people with heart disease. Out in space, nothing has any weight. In space, the muscles in our bodies have very little work to do. The heart is a muscle. So when a person is out in space his heart has less work to do. People with heart disease can be treated successfully in space. In space these people can live longer.'

The Senator remembered his last meeting with Dr Harkness. He had stopped the doctor's research in space medicine. He remembered the scene. He had questioned the doctor at the meeting:

'Why do you want so much money, Dr Harkness? Many people are worried about your research work. Why do you want to send so many people into space? It is dangerous. Already, men have died. We don't want to lose more lives.'

Dr Harkness had tried to explain his plans. He wanted to learn more about medicine in space. In space, nothing has any weight. Perhaps sick people could be cured when they were weightless. But Dr Harkness did not explain his plans well. The Senator had laughed at him. The Government had not given him more money for his research.

Senator Steelman was unhappy when he remembered this last meeting with Dr Harkness.

'Why are you telling me this?' he asked. 'I only want to die quietly.'

'But there is hope for you,' said Dr Harkness. 'The Russians want to cure you. You are a famous man.'

In the end, the Senator went to Russia. At the Satellite Hospital of the USSR, he waited in a room with other sick people. He saw a young man and woman. They looked very young and very much in love with each other. They were looking at each other with tears in their eyes.

Which of them is dying? the Senator asked himself. He felt sorry for them. They were so young.

The nurse called the Senator into the doctor's room.

A few days later, the Senator returned to Washington. A crowd of reporters and newsmen was waiting for him at the airport.

They all asked questions at the same time.

'How do you feel, Senator?'

'Will you be back at work soon?'

'Are the Russians going to cure you?'

The Senator thought for a moment, then answered slowly and carefully: 'The Russian doctors *think* that they can cure me. But it is not certain.'

'How long will the treatment take?'

'Perhaps six months,' he replied.

'So you won't be President next year. But you'll be ready for the elections in four years' time.'

The Senator waited a moment before he replied.

'I need more time before I can answer your question,' he said. 'I can't tell you anything now.' He turned and saw his wife and Joey and Susan. The children ran to him and hugged him. In his heart he already knew his answer.

Some days later, the Senator had a talk with Dr Harkness and the Russian Director of the Satellite Hospital. He could see them both on the screens in his office.

Dr Harkness spoke first, from the right-hand screen.

'Everything is ready for you, Senator. They are waiting for you at the Satellite Hospital.'

The children ran to him and hugged him.

The Senator turned to the left-hand screen and spoke to the Russian professor.

'Professor, may I ask you a question? Many people want to be treated in your Satellite Hospital. How do you choose your patients? Why do you treat some patients and not others? How many patients can you take?'

'Well,' said the Russian slowly. 'Not many. In fact, fewer than ten.'

The Senator knew the thoughts of both Dr Harkness and the Russian. Dr Harkness wanted to show the American people that space medicine was important. Then the American Government would give him money for his research. The Russian professor wanted to cure this famous American politician. He wanted the whole world to praise Russia. He wanted the whole world to know about the success of Russian scientific research.

But the Senator was thinking of something very different. He was thinking of that young couple in the waiting-room. One of them was going to die if he went to the Satellite Hospital.

'Thank you very much, gentlemen,' he said. 'But I cannot go to the Satellite Hospital. Thank you both.'

He switched off the screens and felt very happy.

Soon it was summer. One day, he went with his wife and grandchildren to visit the White House. It was the home of the President of the USA. It was a beautiful and peaceful place. He took the children through the rooms and answered all their questions. After a while, he began to feel tired and wanted to rest.

'Take the children to see the other rooms,' he told his wife. 'I'll wait for you outside.'

'Are you feeling all right?' she asked.

'I'm all right. I just want to sit down and rest for a few moments.'

His wife took the children to see the other rooms. The Senator watched the River Potomac. It flowed slowly past towards the great ocean. Senator Steelman felt at peace. He no longer wanted to be President of the United States. He had found happiness. He was thankful.

As he sat there, Death came to take him, softly and without pain or fear.

BEFORE EDEN

'We can't go any further,' said Jerry Garfield.

He stopped the engines of the scout car. They were not far from the South Pole on the planet of Venus. In front of them, there was a high cliff. The scout car could not climb the rocky cliff.

'We'll have to go back,' Jerry said to the others.

The other two men were scientists. They wanted to explore the South Pole of Venus. They did not want to go back. Hutchins looked carefully at the cliff through his binoculars.

'Look!' he said. 'Do you see that?'

Coleman looked through his binoculars.

'At one time, water has run down that cliff,' said Hutchins. 'We're looking at a dried-up waterfall! I was right. There are rivers on Venus.' He was very excited.

'How can there be any rivers?' asked Jerry. 'There's no water on Venus. It's too hot on this planet for rain to fall. There's no water here at all.'

'But it's colder here near the South Pole. And it will be colder up on the cliff. Up there, it will be cold enough for rain to fall. We must get to the Pole.'

'Why?' asked Jerry.

'If there is water,' replied Hutchins, 'perhaps there will be something living in it. If there are lakes up there, I want to look at them.'

'But we can't get up there in the car,' said Jerry.

'We'll have to leave the car and climb the cliff,' said Hutchins. 'It won't be too difficult.'

Coleman stayed behind, and Hutchins and Jerry set off for the cliffs. It was hard work. The temperature outside was two hundred and thirty degrees. They had to wear their refrigerated spacesuits, and they had to carry scientific equipment.

As they climbed, the green light of Venus shone around them. At the top of the cliff, the ground became flat. They could see the marks of dried-up rivers. They walked on and on. Jerry began to feel afraid, but Hutchins was excited. He stopped to collect pieces of rock.

'It's getting colder,' Hutchins said. 'My instruments tell me that there's oxygen in the atmosphere.'

'What does that mean?' asked Jerry.

'That means there are plants here,' explained Hutchins. 'Plants make oxygen. That means that there is life on Venus. It is not a dead planet.'

They walked on. Soon they saw a lake of water ahead of them. It looked like a black mirror. Hutchins collected a few drops of water and looked at them through his microscope. But he could not see any living thing in the drops of water.

They went on. Jerry felt more and more unhappy. He did not like the place at all. The green light and the black lake made the place strange and frightening.

Suddenly Hutchins stopped.

'What's the matter?' asked Jerry.

'Look at that rock,' said Hutchins. 'It's growing. It's growing bigger and it's moving.'

Jerry looked at the rock. The dark shape moved. It was coming towards them. Hutchins watched through the binoculars. The rock crept closer and closer. When it was about a hundred yards away from them, Jerry spoke.

'What is it?' he asked.

The dark shape moved. It was coming towards them.

'It's a plant of some kind,' said Hutchins.

'But it's moving! Plants can't move!'

'Yes, they can,' said Hutchins. 'There are plants on Earth that move. But very slowly. This one certainly moves fast!'

The plant was like a thick, black, soft carpet. It moved silently towards them. Then about ten feet away from them, it stopped. Hutchins stepped forward. The plant moved back.

'It can feel the heat from our spacesuits,' said Hutchins. He took out a torch. 'Does it feel light too?'

When he switched on the torch, both men cried out in astonishment. In the green light of Venus, the plant looked black. In the white light of the torch, the plant was fiery red and gold. It was like a beautiful carpet.

Hutchins wanted to examine the plant more closely. He tried to cut off a small piece of the plant. It was difficult to get hold of it. But, at last, he was able to cut off a piece. Then he collected some of the rocks. It was hard work and the two men were getting tired in their heavy spacesuits.

They decided to have a rest. They put up their small tent and lay down inside. Both of them were very excited. Everyone had called Venus 'the dead planet'. But they had discovered life. Venus had life on it – like Earth and Mars.

It was time to leave. They collected their rubbish and put it into a plastic bag. They dug a hole and put the bag in it. They covered the hole with stones. Then they set off back towards the cliff. After a few hours, they reached the scout car. They planned to make another visit soon to the South Pole of Venus.

For a while, nothing moved near the lake. Then another plant appeared. It moved over the stones. It was looking for food. Something was there, something was beneath the stones. The plant searched among the stones, and at last it found the plastic bag.

The plant opened the bag easily and sucked up the rubbish inside. And with the rubbish, it sucked up tiny living creatures. It sucked up those tiny creatures that cause disease on Earth. We call them bacteria and viruses. Some were still alive in the rubbish.

The plant moved slowly back to the lake. And with it, it took the diseases that were going to destroy all life on Venus. Jerry and Hutchins did not know what they had done. They had destroyed life on Venus. Venus would become a dead planet once more.

DOG STAR

In my sleep, I heard Laika. She was barking. Then I woke up and remembered. Laika was dead. She had died five years ago on Earth. And I was in my cabin on the Observatory on the Moon.

I had found Laika years ago. I had found her on the road to the Observatory at Palomar in the United States. She was very small and frightened. I was afraid that a car would run over her. So I picked her up. I did not like animals very much. So I planned to give her to a friend. But then she opened her eyes and looked up at me. I fell in love with her.

So she stayed with me. She was a beautiful Alsatian dog and very intelligent. When I went to work, she came with me. She always lay quietly in a corner while I worked at the big telescope in Palomar.

One day, I had to go to Berkeley. I didn't want to leave Laika behind, so I took her in the car. My friends didn't like dogs, but they allowed her to sleep in the sitting-room.

'She's a good dog,' I told them. 'She won't make a noise.'

But, in the middle of the night, she began to make a lot of noise. What can be wrong? I wondered. I went to the sitting-room. Laika was barking and scratching at the door.

'Shut up, Laika!' I said. 'I'll let you out. But don't bark so loudly.'

I opened the door and she raced outside. It was a warm night, so I waited for her outside the house.

Then something strange happened. The earth began to

move. I heard crashes and bangs all around. It was an earthquake. The houses all round me began to fall down. My friends' house fell on top of them. They were killed. But I was safe. A helicopter came to rescue me. But I refused to go.

'I must find my dog,' I told the helicopter pilot. He thought that I was mad. But I found her.

After that, Laika and I were always together. But then I was offered an important job – Chief Astronomer at the Observatory on the Moon! I couldn't take Laika with me to the Moon. I had to choose between Laika and my job – and it wasn't an easy choice.

In the end, I gave Laika to some friends and I went off to the Moon. A month later, I heard that she was dead. I had loved Laika and I missed her very much. At first I often dreamt of her. But, as the years passed, I dreamt of her less.

More than a year had passed since I last dreamt of her. So I was surprised when I heard her bark.

Why had I suddenly remembered Laika?

I sat up in bed and tried to think. At that moment, I heard bangs and crashes all around me. The metal wall of my cabin broke open. The air rushed out with a hissing sound. Without thinking, I pressed the alarm button and put on my space helmet. It was an earthquake.

Years ago on the Earth, Laika had saved me from one earthquake. Here on the Moon, she had come to me in a dream. She had saved me from another earthquake. How had she done it? I can't answer that question. But I am grateful to her and I will never forget her.

SATURN RISING

Good evening, ladies and gentlemen.

I met Morris Perlman many years ago. I was twenty-eight years old. I had returned from the first space voyage to Saturn six weeks earlier. I was visiting different parts of America and giving lectures about our journey to Saturn. Everybody wanted to hear me talk about this exciting space voyage.

I was staying at a hotel which was good but not too expensive. That was the kind of hotel I liked.

While I was eating my breakfast in the hotel, a middle-aged man sat down opposite me.

'Good morning,' he said politely. 'I enjoyed your lecture last night.'

I wasn't very pleased. I like to have breakfast alone. I did not want to answer questions about my lecture at that moment.

But Mr Perlman (that was his name) did not want to ask me questions. He wanted to tell me something.

'When I was a boy,' he said, 'I fell in love with Saturn. I saw a picture of this planet. I thought the rings round Saturn were beautiful. I wanted to see Saturn's rings for myself. So I decided to make a telescope. It's very easy, you know. Have you ever made a telescope?'

I shook my head. 'I'm an engineer, not an astronomer,' I said. 'I don't know much about telescopes.'

'Well,' said Mr Perlman, 'I had no money when I was young. But I wanted to see Saturn's rings for myself. So I had to make my own telescope. I got a book from the library and found out how to make a telescope.

'It took me weeks to make a telescope. But, in the end, I was successful.'

I began to feel interested in this man. He was different from other people.

'I remember the night my telescope was ready,' said Mr Perlman. 'I was very excited. That night I was going to look at Saturn through my own telescope! I took the telescope up onto the roof and put it in the right position.

'My father was the manager of a cheap hotel on Third Avenue, New York. The whole family lived and worked in the hotel. We didn't make much money. My father was always worried about money.

'I often helped in the hotel. That evening, it was my turn to help at the reception desk – but I forgot all about it. I was up on the roof with my new telescope.

'The sky was full of stars. It was very hard to find Saturn with my home-made telescope. But, at last, I saw it clearly. I could also see Titan to one side of it. Saturn hung in the dark sky with its wonderful bright rings around it. It was amazing. I sat on the roof for a long time. I had forgotten my father, the hotel and New York.

'But my father hadn't forgotten me. He was looking for me and he was very angry. When my father saw me on the roof he was furious. He grabbed hold of my precious telescope and threw it down. I'll never forget the noise it made as it broke into pieces. That was my first and last telescope. I never made another.

'Of course, it was my fault. It was my turn to help at the reception desk. And my father didn't know that I had made the telescope myself. He didn't know how hard I had worked to make it.'

For a while Mr Perlman was silent. Then he looked at me and smiled.

'Not long after that, things changed,' he went on. 'Dad left home and I became manager of the hotel. That part of town became fashionable and the hotel started to make money. It started to make a lot of money. So I bought another hotel. Then I bought another. Soon I had hotels all across the United States.

'But I've never forgotten Saturn. Your lecture reminded me of when I was a boy. I remembered my first sight of Saturn through my home-made telescope. Let me know when you come back here again. Good luck – and thank you.'

He smiled and went away.

After my breakfast, I asked the waitress who the man was.

'That's Mr Perlman,' said the waitress. 'He owns this hotel.' I asked her to tell me more about him. She told me some very interesting things. Mr Perlman was the most important hotel owner in the United States. He was one of the richest men in the world.

Five years later, I went back to Saturn. We landed on all Saturn's moons and we explored the rings. When I got back to Earth, I gave some more lectures. Once again, I met Mr Perlman. This time, he took me to dinner at a very expensive restaurant. (He owned it, of course.) He asked me all about our journey.

'What is Saturn like?' he asked. 'Is it beautiful?'

'It's like a dream,' I said.

I tried to describe it to him. The huge, golden ball of Saturn itself, the different moons and the great bright rings. The rings were made of floating pieces of ice. Our ship was able to go right into them.

Then Mr Perlman asked me a strange question.

'Which moon,' he asked, 'is the best one to build a hotel on?'

I was amazed at his question.

'But it's impossible in such a place,' I said. 'It's too far away. It would cost far too much to build. And human beings can't even live there yet.'

He smiled at me. 'I can't build it yet,' he said. 'But I will be able to build it in a few years' time. A hundred years ago, people didn't think that men would land on the Moon. But now, men go much further than the Moon in their spaceships. You've been to Saturn. You tell me – which moon shall I build my hotel on?'

I thought carefully.

'Some are too near Saturn. The planet is so large that you can't see anything else. Some moons are too small to live on. The best moon is Titan. You saw Titan with your home-made telescope, didn't you? That's the best place to build a hotel.'

I didn't believe that he would ever build his hotel.

I didn't believe that he would ever build his hotel.

But, ladies and gentlemen, here we are. Yes, you're quite right. Mr Perlman made me the first manager of this hotel on Titan.

Now let's go down to the Observation room. You can watch Saturn rising from there. I still like to watch it – after all these years!

TROUBLE WITH TIME

'We don't have much crime on Mars,' said Detective Inspector Rawlings. 'That's why I'm going back to Earth.'

We were sitting in the departure lounge of the space station. We were on the tiny moon of Mars. Through the windows on one side, we could see the huge shape of the planet Mars. We were waiting for the spaceship which was going to take us back to Earth.

'Sometimes there's an interesting case,' said the Inspector 'You're an art dealer. You buy and sell works of art, don't you, Mr Maccar?' He turned to a small man sitting near him. 'Did you hear about the theft at Meridian City?'

Mr Maccar shook his head. 'I don't think so,' he said.

'Not many people know about it,' said the Inspector. 'A thief from Earth tried to steal the famous statue of the Siren Goddess.'

The statue of the Siren Goddess is about eight inches high and it is made of sandstone. It is very old and very famous. It was kept in the Museum of Meridian City. It was the most valuable thing in the whole Museum. The tourists on Mars buy copies of it to take back to Earth.

'How could anyone steal it?' I asked.

'I'll tell you the story,' said the Inspector. 'Of course, someone was paying the thief. He was doing it for someone – probably for an important art dealer. Danny Weaver (that was the thief's name) was staying in a hotel in Meridian West. He knew that the Museum was closed on Sundays. On Saturday, he walked across the city to Meridian East and went to the Museum. He looked round the Museum.

The statue of the Siren Goddess was in the middle of a large room. Danny Weaver hid in a small room and waited until the Museum closed. The bell rang and the visitors left the Museum. But Danny Weaver stayed hidden. At midnight he started work.'

'But what about the guards?' I asked. 'Didn't they find Danny?'

The Inspector laughed. – They don't have guards on Mars,' he said. 'There's usually no need for them. The officials search your bags when you leave the city. You can't leave with stolen goods.'

That was true. Now I knew why there was no crime on Mars.

'At midnight,' the Inspector went on, 'Danny got out his set of tools. The statue was in a special glass and metal box. He cut all round it very carefully. His plan was very simple. He had a copy of the statue with him. He was going to take out the real statue and put the copy in the box in its place. Then he was going to go back and hide in the small room. On Monday morning, he was going to join the crowds of visitors to the Museum and go out with them.

'Then he got a terrible shock. It was half past eight in the morning and he was not expecting anyone. He knew the Museum was closed on Sundays. But there were noises – the door was opening – the Museum workers came in! Danny dropped his tools and the statue and ran. Out in the street, he got another shock. People were on their way to work. Everyone was busy. What had gone wrong?

'The police found him easily. Only visitors from Earth make that mistake. We have an international dateline on Earth, but it's in the Pacific Ocean. They have a dateline on Mars, too, but it goes through a city – Meridian City. In Meridian West it was Sunday – but in Meridian East it was only Saturday. Danny hadn't thought of that problem. We all felt sorry for Danny.'

Then I asked, 'What happened to Danny?'

'There are no prisons on Mars,' said the Inspector. 'He was given a special job to do for six years. He became a guard at the Museum in Meridian City!'

Danny dropped his tools and the statue and ran.

'And what about the men who were paying him?' I asked. 'Did you catch them?'

'Not yet,' said the Inspector. He turned to the art dealer, Mr Maccar. The art dealer was very quiet. 'Do you think we will catch the men Danny was working for?' the Inspector asked. He looked carefully at Mr Maccar. 'You don't look very well,' he said. 'Would you like one of my space sickness pills, Mr Maccar?'

'No thank you,' said the art dealer. His voice was as cold as ice. It gave me a shock. I looked from him to the Inspector and back again. They both had strange looks on their faces.

This is going to be an interesting journey, I thought to myself, very interesting indeed.

A SLIGHT CASE OF SUNSTROKE

I was a visitor in Perivia. It was the day of the annual football match between Perivia and Panagura. More than a hundred thousand fans were going to the game. I didn't want to go to watch it.

My friend told me about last year's match. It sounded more like a battle than a game of football. Perivia had lost the match. The Perivians said the referee had not done his job properly.

'Why didn't you give the referee a bribe?' I asked.

'We did,' my friend replied. 'We gave him a lot of money. But the Panagurans gave him much more.'

I changed my mind. I went to the match with my friend. The stadium was full of people. The police searched everyone.

The search at the entrance took a long time. The police were looking for dangerous weapons. I bought a programme. It was large, with a silver cover and it was called the Special Victory Souvenir Issue.

How do the Perivians know that they are going to win? I wondered. I began to read my programme. Among other things, it said that the fifty thousand Perivian soldiers in the stadium had free copies of the programme.

Who paid for those fifty thousand copies? I thought.

At last the game began. After half a minute, one of the Perivian players tripped up a Panaguran. The Panaguran fell to the ground. The referee did nothing.

This time, I thought to myself, the Perivians have paid a big enough bribe to the referee.

The players moved quickly down the field. The referee ran after them. He was running slowly. Suddenly I understood what was wrong. Have you ever seen a man trying to run when he is wearing a bullet-proof vest? I can tell you, it isn't easy! I began to feel sorry for the referee.

The game went on peacefully for a time. I began to feel disappointed. Then there was a fight between five players. A few minutes later, four of them were carried off the field.

When the game started again, the Panagurans immediately scored a goal. The crowd roared with rage. A moment later, the referee gave the Panagurans a free kick at goal. They scored: two nil to the Panagurans.

After the first angry roar, the crowd became very still. The silence was frightening. I felt very sorry for that referee. At that moment he was the most hated man in all Perivia.

A few seconds before half-time, Perivia scored a beautiful goal. The referee blew the whistle. I couldn't believe what had happened. The referee had not allowed the goal. The crowd went mad. At last the police calmed them down. The two teams moved back to their own sides of the field. The referee stood all alone in the middle of the field.

I heard the sound of a bugle blowing. Then I heard it again. All at once, the crowd seemed to disappear in a sea of fire. The blinding light hurt my eyes. For a moment, I thought there had been an explosion.

I opened my eyes and looked up. Everything was exactly the same – except for one thing. One man had disappeared. There had been a referee in the middle of that football field. Now there was only a small pile of smoking ashes.

What had happened? I turned to my friend. He was shocked too. But he was looking down at the silver-covered programme on his knee. And then I understood.

All at once, the crowd seemed to disappear in a sea of fire.

There is a lot of power in sunlight. A lot of heat can be reflected from a square of silver. At the sound of the bugle, those fifty thousand soldiers in the crowd had lifted up their programmes. Each programme had reflected the rays of the sun. They had reflected the rays of the sun at the referee.

The heat had burnt him to ashes.

Another referee came onto the football pitch. He did his job properly and the game ended peacefully. The score was 14 – 2 to Perivia. No one seemed sorry for the dead referee. In Perivia, football is a serious business.

Points for Understanding

SUMMERTIME ON ICARUS

1 Colin Sherrard was working with other scientists on Icarus. Why was Icarus the hottest place in the solar system?
2 What happened to Sherrard's space pod when he aimed the pod at the spaceship and fired the jets?
3 Sherrard had to keep his space pod out of the rays of the sun.
   (a) Why?
   (b) How was he able to do this at first?
   (c) What happened when the legs of his space pod broke?
4 When I feel the heat of the sun, I will pull the Emergency Lever, thought Sherrard.
   (a) What would happen when Sherrard pulled the Emergency Lever?
   (b) What did happen?
5 How was Sherrard rescued?

WHO'S THERE?

1 The Station Supervisor had to go outside the space station.
   (a) What did he have to bring in?
   (b) What did he have to put on before he went outside the space station?
2 Who did the Station Supervisor meet on his way to get his spacesuit?
3 I climbed into my spacesuit.
   (a) What was the spacesuit like?
   (b) Why did the Station Supervisor not check the lockers and the food store?
4 Why did the Station Supervisor freeze with fear?
5 Why did the Station Supervisor remember Bernie Summers?
6 Why was 'Tommy' responsible for what happened to the Station Supervisor?

INTO THE COMET

1 George Pickett was speaking into his tape recorder. But he did not think anyone would ever listen to his recording. Why not?
2 Describe Randall's Comet.
3 Why was the *Challenger* trapped in the middle of Randall's Comet?
4 What is an abacus? In what way is it similar to a computer?
5 What was George Pickett's plan? Did it work?

LET THERE BE LIGHT

1 Edgar Burton and his wife, Mary, were a strange couple.
   (a) What was the difference in their ages?
   (b) How did Edgar spend his days and his nights?
   (c) Why was Mary not happy?
2 Mary told Edgar a lie.
   (a) What lie did Mary tell?
   (b) How did Edgar know that Mary was not telling the truth?
   (c) What did Edgar decide was happening between Mary and Rupert de Vere Courtenay?
3 At night, when Mary's car came round a bend in the road, the bright headlights shone right into the house. Why did this make Edgar angry?
4 Edgar planned to murder his wife.
   (a) What was his plan?
   (b) Why did his plan not succeed?
   (c) What happened to Edgar?
   (d) What happened to Mary?

DEATH AND THE SENATOR

1 Why was Senator Steelman planning a holiday for his wife, his daughter and his grandchildren?

2 Dr Harkness visited Senator Steelman.
   (a) Why did Senator Steelman feel unhappy when he remembered his last meeting with Dr Harkness?
   (b) What news did Dr Harkness bring to Senator Steelman?

3 When Senator Steelman was in the waiting room of the Russian Space Hospital, he noticed a young man and woman. They were in love with each other. Why did he feel sorry for them?

4 Dr Harkness wanted Senator Steelman to be cured. So did the Russian professor.
   (a) Why did Dr Harkness want him to be cured?
   (b) Why did the Russian professor want the senator to be cured?

5 Why did Senator Steelman refuse the offer of help from the Russians?

6 How did Senator Steelman die?

BEFORE EDEN

1 Where were Jerry Garfield, Hutchins and Coleman?

2 Hutchins and Coleman were very excited when they saw a dried-up waterfall.
   (a) Why were they excited?
   (b) Why did they both want to reach the South Pole?

3 'My instruments tell me that there is oxygen in the atmosphere,' Hutchins said. Why was that important?

4 When Jerry and Hutchins were near the South Pole, they saw something moving towards them.
   (a) What did it look like?
   (b) What did it do when it got near to them?
   (c) What had they discovered about Venus?

5 What terrible thing did Jerry and Hutchins do before they left Venus?

DOG STAR

1 The person telling this story is the Chief Astronomer in an observatory. Where is the observatory?
2 The Chief Astronomer woke up suddenly when he heard Laika barking. Why was it impossible for the Chief Astronomer to have heard Laika?
3 How had Laika saved the Chief Astronomer's life when he was on earth?
4 What happened when the Chief Astronomer woke up?
5 Why will the Chief Astronomer never forget Laika?

SATURN RISING

1 This story is told in the form of a speech.
   (a) How old was the speaker when he first met Morris Perlman?
   (b) Which planet had the speaker just been visiting?
2 Morris Perlman told the speaker that when he was a boy he fell in love with the planet Saturn.
   (a) What did Morris Perlman think were beautiful?
   (b) Why did Morris Perlman have to make his own telescope?
   (c) What happened to the home-made telescope?
3 The waitress told the speaker more about Morris Perlman. Who was Morris Perlman?
4 Five years later, the speaker returned to Saturn. On his return to Earth, he met Morris Perlman again.
   (a) Who owned the restaurant they went to?
   (b) How did the speaker describe the rings of Saturn?
   (c) What strange question did Morris Perlman ask the speaker?
   (d) What was the speaker's reply?
5 What is the unexpected ending to the speaker's story?

TROUBLE WITH TIME

1 'That's why I'm going back to Earth,' said Detective Inspector Rawlings.
   (a) Where was Inspector Rawlings?
   (b) Why was he going back to Earth?
2 Who was Mr Maccar?
3 What was the Siren Goddess?
4 How did Danny Weaver plan to steal the Siren Goddess?
5 Danny Weaver made a bad mistake about the dateline on Mars. What mistake did he make?
6 Danny Weaver was caught, but the men who were paying him were not caught.
   (a) Why do you think Mr Maccar looked unwell?
   (b) Why do you think it was going to be an interesting journey?

A SLIGHT CASE OF SUNSTROKE

1 The year before, the Perivians had lost the annual football match against the Panagurans. How had the Panagurans made sure the referee was on their side?
2 The visitor bought a programme called the Special Victory Souvenir Issue.
   (a) What was strange about the name of the programme?
   (b) How many Perivian soldiers had been given a free copy of the programme?
   (c) What was the cover of the programme made of?
3 Why was the referee not able to run quickly?
4 A few seconds before half-time, the Perivians scored a goal.
   (a) What did the referee do?
   (b) What did the crowd do?
5 Who was left alone in the middle of the field?
6 The visitor heard the sound of a bugle.
   (a) What hurt the visitor's eyes?
   (b) What happened to the referee?
   (c) How had the Perivians made sure that they would win the game?

A SELECTION OF GUIDED READERS AVAILABLE AT

ELEMENTARY LEVEL

Road to Nowhere *by John Milne*
The Black Cat *by John Milne*
Don't Tell Me What To Do *by Michael Hardcastle*
The Runaways *by Victor Canning*
The Red Pony *by John Steinbeck*
The Goalkeeper's Revenge and Other Stories *by Bill Naughton*
The Stranger *by Norman Whitney*
The Promise *by R.L. Scott-Buccleuch*
The Man With No Name *by Evelyn Davies and Peter Town*
The Cleverest Person in the World *by Norman Whitney*
Claws *by John Landon*
Z for Zachariah *by Robert C. O'Brien*
Tales of Horror *by Bram Stoker*
Frankenstein *by Mary Shelley*
Silver Blaze and Other Stories *by Sir Arthur Conan Doyle*
Tales of Ten Worlds *by Arthur C. Clarke*
The Boy Who Was Afraid *by Armstrong Sperry*
Room 13 and Other Ghost Stories *by M.R. James*
The Narrow Path *by Francis Selormey*
The Woman in Black *by Susan Hill*

For further information on the full selection of Readers at all five levels in the series, please refer to the Macmillan Readers catalogue.

Published by Macmillan Heinemann ELT
Between Towns Road, Oxford OX4 3PP
Macmillan Heinemann ELT is an imprint of
Macmillan Publishers Limited
Companies and representatives throughout the world
Heinemann is a registered trademark of Harcourt Education, used under licence.

ISBN 1–405–07282–2
EAN 978–1–405072–82–3

These stories were first published in 1963 in Great Britain by Victor Gollancz Ltd. They are included in this series by kind permission of Victor Gollancz Ltd

These retold versions by Helen Reid-Thomas for Macmillan Readers
First published 1998

This edition first published 2005

Illustrated by Steve Kyte
Cover photograph by Aaron Horowitz/Corbis

Printed in Thailand

2009 2008 2007 2006 2005
10 9 8 7 6 5 4 3 2